HEALING FROM REGRETS

Guide to Personal Freedom, Overcoming Regrets, Past Mistakes, Stop Worrying and Start Living Your Best Life

Don Wiseman

INTRODUCTION

There is nothing of the sort as an existence with no second thoughts. Regrets is both an inclination and an example of reasoning where one harps on or continually replays and contemplates an occasion, responses or different activities that might have been taken. Second thoughts can become over agonizing weights that meddle with your current bliss, because you regret and limit your future. Ineffective regrets can likewise hold you back from pushing ahead. In the event that you wind up defeat by regrets, distinguish your sensations of disappointment, figure out how to excuse yourself, and continue ahead.

Realize what regrets is. Regrets is a basic perspective or feeling wherein you fault yourself for things that occurred. Productive regrets can assist you with learning change your conduct for what's to come. Unproductive regrets, where you totally fault yourself, can make constant pressure which prompts medical conditions. Regrets can be over things you have done or not done. For instance, you could regrets acting a specific way during a contention, or you may lament not taking a proposition for employment.

 Recognize your sensations of disappointment. These might be unique in relation to individual to individual, however sensations of disappointment include: pity, misfortune, regret, outrage, disgrace, and uneasiness. Distinguish these sentiments identified with lament. For instance, you may have the prospect of a past deed and afterward you consider this occasion for most of the day. This can leave you feeling crushed and miserable.

 You may consider what you did or said, or you may consider what you wished you had done any other way to change your present circumstance. Steady reevaluating and lamenting can cause uneasiness. This may prompt agonizing over future choices that you may lament later.

CHAPTER ONE

UNDERSTANDING REGRETS

Think about where your regret comes from. Consider what's causing your regrets. Individuals can feel remorseful for various reasons. Ordinary regretful encounters include:

-Way of life: Numerous individuals regret moving to an alternate nation or may wish they hadn't killed a house offer. For instance, you moved from Canada to Australia since you needed a hotter life. However, only months after the fact, you have thought that it was difficult to look for some kind of employment, have encountered life in the city and feel achy to visit the family each and every day. You wish you hadn't took the action down under.

-Work: Individuals may lament not after an alternate profession way and seeking after their fantasy occupations. Or then again they may regret turning down propositions for employment or advancements. For instance, you fear going into your office work regular and often wish you had not turned down the chance to be a co-proprietor in your own business.

-Family: Individuals may lament not resolving questions with a relative or companion, particularly if the other individual passed. Or on the other hand they may regret not investing more energy with more established relatives. For instance, you got the nation over for your companion's work. You never put forth sufficient attempt to remain associated with your grandma through calls or visits. Since your grandma has passed, you regret not investing more energy into remaining associated.

-Kids: Individuals may regret beginning a family. For instance, you began a family since you needed to make your companion's little glimpse of heaven. After 1 year, you are getting no satisfaction from parenthood and your relationship with your accomplice has languished over it, you wish every day you had become a canine encourage like you needed to. Remember nonetheless that numerous Mother and Fathers experience post birth anxiety following the introduction of a child, get proficient assistance in the event that you figure you may have this.

-Marriage: Individuals may regret the circumstance of their marriage or their decision of accomplice. Some may even regret getting hitched by any means. For instance, you wedded your better half/spouse in light of the fact that your family loved and supported them. Following 5 years of marriage, you have discovered that you share no interests. You regularly consider what your life would have been similar to on the off chance that you had hitched your long-lasting young lady/sweetheart who your folks didn't care for.

CHAPTER TWO

OVERCOMING REGRET USING COGNITIVE-BEHAVIORAL THERAPY

1

Utilize Cognitive- Behavioral Therapy (CBT): CBT practices help you to change your propensities and examples of reasoning. You can before long beginning changing your sensations of disappointment, disgrace, and outrage. All things being equal, you'll center on genuinely recuperating any destructive, useless considerations you have.

CBT attempts to lessen and supplant your sensations of disappointment and tension, rather than essentially enlightening yourself to quit thinking regarding the past. This assists you to manage the regrets in a superior manner.

2

Record your second thoughts. With regrets, individuals regularly wonder why they acted or didn't act, and this is frequently where individuals become stuck. Rundown your second thoughts and any inquiries you hush up about posing. For instance, you may ask why you acted the manner in which you did. Go through your rundown and change the why inquiries into what's next? This will assist you with beating the sensation of being trapped.

For instance: You may ask yourself, for what reason did I snap at my kid such a lot of last week? For what's next? You could say that you realize you have almost no persistence left after work. Later on you could enjoy a brief reprieve prior to connecting with the kids.

3

Get familiar with your exercise. Second thoughts can be significant learning devices for what's to come. Attempt to search for the exercises learned and perceive that life exercises make you more astute. For instance, in the event that you lament not approaching your mate with deference, you may have discovered that affronting your mate causes you to feel horrendous. Having this information makes you a more astute mate and individual.

4

Apply what you've realized. What you regret may likewise be things you have found out about yourself as well as other people. Having this information diminishes the shots at settling on a comparative decision later on. Try to apply the insight you've acquired.

For instance, on the off chance that you've discovered that affronting your mate causes your life partner to feel skeptical, don't repeat the experience later on.

5

Control how regrets impact your future. While you cannot change what occurred previously, you can pick how your previous influences your present and future.

For instance, you can't change how a lot or how frequently you drank in school, yet you can settle on the decision not to allow the lament to cause you to feel regretful now or let it influence your future decisions.

6

Perceive productive regret: Thrashing yourself over things outside your ability to control would be viewed as inefficient lament. However, useful lament can be positive in the event that you are moved to work on yourself or follow up on promising circumstances. When you're mindful of a botched chance, be it instructive, monetary, or enthusiastic, you're bound to address the misstep later on.

In the event that you get yourself conflicted about pursuing another open door, inquire as to whether you'd prefer stress over a squandered chance or take a risk. By taking a stab at something new, you're limiting future second thoughts.

CHAPTER THREE

WAYS TO DEAL WITH REGRETS

1

Build compassion for other people. You're not by any means the only one inclination remorseful about something. Consider what others might be going through. Recollect that compassion assists you with bettering comprehend the sensations of others. This may expect you to challenge your own biases and really pay attention to others.

For instance, on the off chance that you lament hefty drinking during your years in school, you may have a profound comprehension of how you child feels following a night he's not pleased with.

2

Transform regret into appreciation. You may consider lament as far as the accompanying proclamations: "I ought to have...." "I could have...." "I can't really accept that I...." "For what reason didn't me....." Change these assertions into explanations of appreciation. You'll consider the past contrastingly and begin to lose the lament. At the point when you discover yourself thinking a remorseful assertion, change it to an assertion of appreciation. This can help you begin contemplating the past in a positive light.

For instance, change "I ought to have attended a university," to "I'm thankful it's not very late to set off for college." Or change "I might have invested more effort to quit drinking," to "I'm appreciative that I can attempt to improve now."

3

Practice self-forgiving: Regret can cause hatred towards yourself as well as other people. All things considered, figure out how to excuse yourself. Not exclusively will this decrease your sensations of disappointment, yet it can work on your confidence. Sound confidence is basic to numerous parts of your life, including connections.

Don't just attempt to eliminate the lament. All things considered, own up to your slip-ups and sentiments, however permit yourself to continue ahead.

4

Write of yourself a letter: The activity of composing a letter will help you work on excusing yourself. This passionate and intellectual instrument will begin to recuperating your sensations of disappointment. Compose a letter addressed to your more youthful or past-self and in the letter converse with your more youthful self like you may converse with your kid or dear companion. This will ensure that you are sympathetic towards yourself.

Remind you're more youthful self that you merit the best in life regardless of whether you committed errors, since you are human and it is alright to commit errors.

5

Practice every day affirmations. An affirmation is a positive assertion to support, elevate you, and make you more empathetic towards yourself.

Having empathy for yourself makes it simpler to sympathize pardon your past-self, which can lessen sensations of disappointment. Advise yourself, compose, or think the certifications. A few instances of assertions include:

-I'm a decent individual and merit the best regardless of my past.

-I'm human and commit errors, and that is alright.

-I have taken in a great deal from quite a while ago, and I'm deserving of a brilliant future.

Not all connections last—some are a greater amount of the learning love kind. Be that as it may, separations are once in a while simple. As a sex advisor and relationship master turned neuroscientist, I frequently hear from individuals who lament separating. It's what I call a separation headache: when we wind up being inundated with sensations of disappointment in the wake of choosing to relinquish a relationship.

Having laments post breakup doesn't really imply that you ought to reunite with your ex. We're wired to feel awful when we experience the departure of a relationship, regardless of whether we're the person who started the separation. Yearning, bitterness, and melancholy are largely flawlessly wired into our enthusiastic senses, and they can help us incline toward accomplishing crafted by development personally. That is uplifting news! Lament is important for lamenting, and as I like to say, breakdown frequently implies forward leap.

CHAPTER FOUR

STEP BY STEP INSTRUCTIONS TO RECOGNIZE IF YOU HAVE REGRETS

On the potential gain of new love, we consider that individual constantly—and those idea circles can be exceptionally intriguing and pleasurable. Yet, significantly affected by new love, our internal exchange can resonate with concerns, fears, and stresses over apparent dangers to the relationship. We are animals of connection, and misfortune poses a potential threat for us.

At the point when we separate, it's not uncommon to encounter a comparable sort of rumination, specifically when we aren't feeling finished and there's more work yet to be finished. It's not unexpected, as such, to lament separating—regardless of whether you're the person who did the unloading. Relationship recuperating, it just so happens, is an inside work that requirements to happen regardless of whether the specific relationship doesn't proceed.

The most effective method to deal with separation

1. Get inquisitive.

Ask yourself these inquiries: Was separating an in-the-second choice? Or then again was it's anything but a more drawn out time? Is life better after the separation? More regrettable? Unaltered? Was the relationship not working in light of the fact that the accomplice was not treating you appropriately?

Try not to be reluctant to get criticism from individuals who know you well. How could they see you reflected in the relationship?

2. Take a relationship stock.

In case you're actually looking for clearness, think back. Were there any signs or indications of an unfortunate relationship? Without allocating fault, see what elements prompted your relationship disappointment and impacted your choice to leave. Is it safe to say that you were or your accomplice critical? Did you not assume the best about one another? Did you not suitably stand firm for what you required in the relationship? Did you will in general make your accomplice wrong when the greater part of what couples quarrel over is only a question of assessment? Assume full liability as far as it matters for you of the dance.

As I tell couples in directing, we each have 100% obligation regarding what appears in a relationship. That is extraordinary information, since that implies we can change things for ourselves going ahead.

3. Try not to whip yourself.

It's totally normal to have regrets regardless of whether you realize the separation is the best thing for you. Perceive that what you're feeling is typical and doesn't really mean you settled on some unacceptable choice. Try not to thrash yourself.

This is a happy chance to rehearse revolutionary acknowledgment. The capacity to endure our sentiments, even the difficult ones, is an indication of passionate wellbeing and an essential expertise for great connections.

4. Get insightful.

As a rule, would you say you are a restless individual who keeps an eye on self-question? What's more, provided that this is true, is the issue truly lament about the deficiency of the relationship or essentially worries about your own dynamic?

Or on the other hand, in case you're as a rule totally fair, do you see an example rehashing across your connections? Do you will in general settle on choices from instabilities or fears? Assuming this is the case, set aside effort to investigate your connection style just as the specific way you see your own necessities and expect how willing others will be to help you meet them. To plunge much more profound, read my book Why Great Sex Matters to assist you with bettering and work your own connection wiring.

5. Utilize this energy to foster yourself.

Examine a portion of these relationship abilities that individuals who do connections adequately practice. Fortunately these abilities can be acquired. Every relationship holds a chance to study yourself and how to join forces with another.

6. Separate it and leap forward.

Through understanding parts of your own social guide, you can turn into a more complete individual going ahead. One device is to consider how we, as a culture, see what we expect of ourselves and one another. Notwithstanding your sex or sexual direction, there are power battles that go on in our connections that are intensely impacted by old, obsolete ideas of sex jobs and assumptions that drive struggle. So for instance, in the event that you will in general believe you must support (normally female job), and you're not sustaining yourself, you'll most likely foster disdain. In like manner, if your accomplice believes you must do the greater part of the hard work to accommodate your family (regularly manly job) and you don't, they'll presumably loathe you.

In the event that you will in general be incautious and race right into it without thought, you may rush to cut off a friendship and continue onward. Thus laments. One part of our social selves that could be better evolved in us everything is the "uninvolved" job or the capacity to notice ourselves and each other with interest and knowledge, without racing right into it or response.

Most importantly the more cognizant and more adaptable we are about what we expect of ourselves and one another, the better connections will stream.

7. Finally accept reality for what it is.

Since you have a superior handle on what prompted the separation, consider putting together a discussion with your ex to investigate what should be done with the end goal for you to leave feeling more complete with the relationship. Check whether you can figure out how to give up with adoration.

On the off chance that that is impractical to do face to face, you can finally accept reality with the accomplice by recording your considerations and sentiments, joining what you've realized. You can send the letter (or not). The main thing is getting clear on your own development through this experience with the goal that you are one bit nearer to making enduring affection.

CHAPTER FIVE

BEST WAYS TO DEAL WITH REGRETS

Regrets is perhaps the most remarkable human feelings. It is hard to neglect and extreme to survive. However when left unchecked, lament can become incapacitating. It can secure you inside your own brain, burdening you with dread, outrage, and misery. In spite of the difficulties, then, at that point, it is vital to discover approaches to manage lament and continue forward from it.

Here are six scientifically demonstrated approaches to do precisely that.

1. Discover the Exercise

At its center, lament can be seen as your brain ruminating over a botched chance. Regardless of whether you didn't accomplish something and presently wish that you had, or you accomplished something and presently wish that you hadn't, your decision of activity or inaction straightforwardly prompted the inclination you are currently encountering. Set aside some effort to sit with that acknowledgment.

Thoroughly consider the conditions under which you settled on the decision that you made. What was your expected result? What outside factors impacted your choice? Did you, where it counts, accept that your decision was the awesome, just the least demanding? Returning to the circumstance with the advantage of knowing the past can lead you to a more profound comprehension of your dynamic interaction and the things that are genuinely imperative to you, eventually directing you toward better decisions later on.

2. Track down the Silver Lining

Each choice has a heap of results, both great and awful. At the point when you have lament, the adverse results become stuck at the bleeding edge of your brain. However ordinarily, we can straightforwardly follow something great that is going on now to an apparently helpless decision previously.

What was probably going to occur assuming you had settled on an alternate choice back? What undoubtedly would NOT have occurred? Obviously, this progression requires a lot of hypothesis, since nobody truly realizes what every little choice means for the course of her life. In any case, searching out the decency that came from a lamented choice can help you discover viewpoint and understand that things do have a method of turning out to be a good thing.

3. Forgive Yourself

A lot of the agony of disappointment is established in self-fault and outrage. However just knowing the past is 20/20. Everything considered, it could be extremely simple to see where you turned out badly. At the time, in any case, you were doing all that could be expected with the data that you had at that point. Excuse yourself for being a defective human, and you will go far toward conquering lament.

4. Embrace Change

People will in general get a feeling of harmony and strength from carrying on with an anticipated life. However nothing is sure in life except for change. In some cases regret is stirred up with pain over losing an individual or circumstance that felt agreeable and secure. However there are definitely no ensures that whatever you lament is the lone explanation that your life has changed.

Life is comprised of an apparently interminable number of little decisions, and just seldom does a solitary occasion shift its whole direction. On the off chance that you can figure out how to accept change, or if nothing else acknowledge its certainty, then, at that point this part of disappointment will disappear.

5. Become More Versatile

Connected at the hip with accepting change is figuring out how to adjust to the moving breezes. Set aside some effort to break down the thing is keeping you down, and put forth a conscious attempt on figuring out how to conquer it. The more versatile you can turn into, the more regret will blur out of spotlight as you assume the difficulties of new experiences.

6. Focus on the future

Eventually, there is no way to change the past, and regret just keeps you stuck looking in reverse. Take a stock of your life as it as of now exists, and the things that you need to anticipate. Discover approaches to break out of a trench, plan energizing new encounters with your loved ones, and begin running after your greatest dreams. With such a huge amount on your plate, the agony of disappointment will before long be substituted by trust for what's to come.

Regret is an incredible feeling, and it is not difficult to stall out in a pattern of dread and trouble. Following these six hints, nonetheless, will assist you with taking in what you can from the past.